DEATH OF A SNOWMAN

What the puddle had to say…

Poems by
Raundi K. Moore-Kondo

❅

Death of a Snowman
What the puddle had to say...

Wake Up! appears in Lummox Vol. III on Lummox Press
Melting and *Gag Order* both appear in
Cadence Collective online and in Cadence Collective Vol. II
*Recovered Dental Records Will Indicate Cause Of Death: Lack Of
A Heart* contains ghost lines by JL Martindale,
G. Murray Thomas and Daniel McGinn

Cover art by Raundi Kai Moore-Kondo
Cover layout by Savanah R. Moore-Kondo

ISBN-13:
978-0692488096 (For The Love Of Words)
ISBN-10:
069248809X

For

snowmen

harmed

by

poetry…

DEATH OF A SNOWMAN

What the Puddle Had to Say...

Yours Was the Cool Kiss

The one capable of keeping me awake
night after night for the rest of my life

The one that would nag at me
not to give up

The one that traced my lips
with such deliberate delicacy
they could no longer bear another's touch

They could no longer form words

My lips were left pursed

Partially open

Lying in wait

For yours was the only kiss
that would forever
matter

My Heart Just Gasmed

It leapt with

Joy!

Bliss

YES!

Now

Amen and Halleluiah

to its little death

A part of
me

lost
forever

Reborn
as a spark of

Us

Stop the Brilliance

Stop shining so bright
and keeping me awake

Make it stop

I only want to fly directly
into your incandescence

I can't resist your moonlight

My wings will fry
My insides will internally combust

Turn it down
I am trying to sleep

Turn down
I am trying to stay alive

Turn down
I can't love you more than I already do

Turn down
It is too much
I am going blind

Please!

Love, turn down
Before I turn to magic smoke

If You Are Not Man,
I Am Not Woman

I am everything you are not
and more
All the soft you have been afraid
to allow

I am sub-sonic; frequencies so high
your dog can't hear me

A ninja stirring
good morning cream
and buttering bread

Brain food, solar power, and Earth

I am wind
and dependable eye of the hurricane

A witness to your struggle
I am the burning match

Come to me
I am the only drowning
that quenches

I hear all and will show you
everything

Without you,
I am nothing

Come In

Where thick and rich simmer
And gooey-sweet warm bakes

And the tea...
Well the tea is always just the way you like it

The fire is lit and the lights are dim

Come in

The blankets are French toast soft
and the sheets are Columbian roast smooth

Come in

The music is made by lips
and powered by breath

Come in

It is cold out there

Come in

Where the wind cannot find you
Where the snow will envy you

Come in

Food For Lips

You
maple and smoke
lime and brown sugar
snowflakes
latex, silver, porcelain
ghost peppers, whispers
hot hallowed jalapeño
Icy whiskey sip
long, slow, cool-wet whistle
Pinotnoirstrawberrylipgloss hum Kashmir
Portuguese tied by cherry-red Neruda tongue
Honeycomb, honey drips and aftershave
Peach fuzzy-navel with cream
Five o'clock shadow
Pillow-Mint-midnight meow

Goodnight tongue

Yes

Oh, yes

Yes

You

Aubade So Bad

I want to write an aubade
to you
so bad
it hurts

My brain is cramping
The spot under my sternum—
just to the right
has developed a piercing stab

My guts stretch themselves
too thin
reaching out to you

my fingers panic
and long to claw
their way out of
this nothing

You will be up soon
and I have nothing to show
for how hard I have missed you

No way to account
for all the time I have already
labored over our love
today

Wake Up!

You are burning moonlight
The sun and its day are on their way

Wake up and remember –
Who you are
Who I am
And who we can be
when we are together

Open your eyes
Prick up your ears
and spread your arms wide

Bare your barrel chest
It was built for more than beating
and target practice

Expose your exquisite throat
Let me hear you howl
at your new found heaven

God, how I miss your song

Wake up!

I am dying to feast
on the whites of your eyes
and feel the mercy of your wet
breath inside my lungs

This All Could Be Yours

The curb appeal
The oh-so welcome mat
All the slick French entryways
The plush lawn and ever-fragrant green
   trimmed and mowed
A garden of plump and lush
Every drop of dew
All of this home-sweet-honey home
The cool breeze and the tickle of ruffled
   curtain cuddling an overstuffed love seat
   next to the window
Giggles muffled by soft radio
The sounds and scents of coffee
And baking cinnamon becoming saffron
And red, red wine
And fire.
All the crackle between the bricks
Banked by the summoning stairs
The calling comforter
The whisper of pillow
The calm of clean walls, fresh paint
   and spiked nightcaps
The built-in toothbrush holder
The extra-sturdy tile counter
   and shiny, polished chrome
The full of the moon in the skylight
The dawn
And the good morning
You are home
   Kiss

17

Let's Get Out Of Here

If we decide to hike
The weather will surely turn torrential and deadly
If we decide to take a short cut we will get lost
And will never be seen from, again
If we take the scenic route
We won't survive the photos
If we go by sea
We drown
If we go by air
We will fall to our deaths, screaming like banshees
If we wear parachutes
We will only become tangled in the lines and fall
  to our deaths, screaming like tangled Banshees
If we are carried off by long toothed predators
  back to their nests
We will be torn limb from limb
And eaten alive by their hunger pained young
Unless, we are dropped and fall to our deaths first
Then we will be eaten after we are found dead
If we eat before we leave
We will be poisoned
If we rest before we leave
We will be attacked in our sleep by savages
Or damned in our dreams to a life of crime
If we slip out the back
We will most likely fall into quicksand, or else
We will be ambushed and scalped
If we hide in the bushes in the backyard
We will be killed by killer bees
Or struck by lightening.

If we stay here we are
trapped and as good as dead—

No matter what we do
This story ends badly
But, if we get back to the porch
before the streetlights come on
We might just be okay for tonight

Buried Treasure

It is deep
It will take some muscle to get it out
There is the possibility of digging to our deaths
And that would only be after we found the spot
The one with the invisible "X"
Which is tricky to get to
And by tricky
I mean we must drown in each other's dementia
Revive our selves in another dimension
Keep quiet and keep moving
It could mean wandering this barren land
  in circles for the rest of our years
An endless string of nights
  spent never sleeping long enough to dream, again
We could become a daily nightmare
The only map has been burnt
Put away wet
And was always smudged and difficult to read
But it's mostly stored in my memory
The landmarks may no longer exist
And the land is plagued with plagues
Fire storms, faulty foot holds
Little to no cover
And bands of roving drunk chimpanzees
armed with hand grenades and kitchen knives
But...there is treasure beneath us!

Treasure, I tell you!
Somewhere

Love, I Get Lost Easily

Don't dare to take your eyes
off me

Buy some binoculars
a magnifying glass, microscope
and maybe a magic mirror
that allows you to see where
I am
at every second
of every day

I'm prone to running
And, hiding
And, never coming back

You should hold my hand
while we are crossing the street
or grocery shopping

Frankly, blinders blunt objects
and a leash might be best

If you must leave me behind
for a bit, tie me to a really tall tree
surrounded by barbed-wired, electric fence,
a deep moat of starved piranha,
and armed guards
facing North, South, East, West,
Heaven, Hell and Oz
Put some flying monkeys in the sky and a

microchip under my skin
Solitary confinement might be best
A dark hole under an active volcano

Or else keep me in your pocket
The one over your heart
Just don't forget to remove me
before you put it in the wash

You Told Me It Was My Turn

This game doesn't fit in a box
It doesn't include dice,
cards, or piles of counterfeit cash
No spinning wheels
or colored pylons
No racecars, dogs,
wheelbarrows, tiny irons
or battleships that I can find
Not even a board
or visible sheet to score

It has no official rules
No way to cheat
No winner
No loser
Or cat's games allowed

I can't stop playing

There is no 800 number
for those who think
they have a problem

There is only you
and, now you refuse to play

I Make Believe In Us

In eye contact, the truth and their light
and gut feelings
Past lives and somehow both happenstance
and kismet

I believe in love at first glimmer
And the security of fool's gold
I believe in the magic
of firsts, lasts, and forevers

The first smile
The first scent of curious
The first words
The first case of butterflies

The first
I have to get know you better

The first
I have to see you, again.
Right NOW!

The first
I have to touch you
I have to kiss you
I have to rip your clothes off

The first
I love you—

The first
This is the last

The first doubt
The first fearful lack of response
The last words of regret
The last time you promised
there wouldn't be a last,
if you could help it—

The last of my self-respect

The last time I believed
everything was okay…

It was maybe just that first day
back when I believed
that eye contact and forever
was enough

Habit Trail

Stop pretending
that you are trapped
in a plastic bubble

I will stop imagining
myself a lonely weaver
whose bed is a deadly web

This is not my only means of survival

Our love is a circus
Sideshow material, at best

You are no tiger
This is not a whip in my mouth

My kiss is a cyanide capsule
When did we become a death match?

Maybe you are not a man
Maybe I am not a woman
Maybe this is not fear

Maybe it is just hunger

Or deadly thirst

Maybe, I am the spider
And you a trapped rat—

We don't speak the same language
These are all just guesses of the freakish

The one with eight arms
to hold you with

Keep running blind
I will wait

You will hit a wall and sleep
That is when we will see
what venom and mercy can do

I Call This a Wall

You said I was wrong
You didn't have another word for it
But, it definitely wasn't a wall

When I pointed to the window
You said "Don't get so excited.
It's only a transparent door."

When I declared it was a masterpiece
You thought it might look nice lining a bird cage

I called it love
You called it a fire escape

I made a promise
You put on a pair of broken handcuffs

I said a prayer
You cursed the night

I phone
You never pick up

I told you it was my whole life
You only cared about the state of the refrigerator

You were a witness to my dream-come true
Then laughed like it was Saturday morning
cartoons

When I called this home
You knew it was a time bomb
and said nothing

Your Concerned Face Speaks
a Thousand Deaths

"The problem is..."
"You just shouldn't"
"You can't possibly"
"Never will"
"Never could"
"No one ever has"
"Don't waste your time"
"Why would anyone want to?"
"If someone does, it won't be you"
"But if somehow you do,
 you'll only live to regret it"
"No chance. No how. No Way"
"God forbid"
"You will only grow more deaf, dumb, and blind."
"How can you do this to me?
 To your loving family?"
"What will your friends think?"
"You'll die broke and alone"
"Everyone will laugh"
"We'll all feel bad we hadn't done more"
"We'll all say we told you so"
"We'll never let you forget it"
"You are more damaged than anyone imagined"
"Such a pity"
"Of course, I still love you,
 anyway"

No Promises

This place is fertile
filthy rich
and fallow

You plant nothing—
for you know that it will only live
to die
under your watch

There were plans
for this plot

Promises of
a promised land

I wished on a breeze
to bring feral seed
and prayed rain was on its way

A volunteer is pushing
through
You take no chances
on chance
You cannot handle
that kind of responsibility

You keep you eyes closed
As your frozen fingers grip the stem
and rip the roots from
our land

Melting

I feel your confusion
It sits on your head
like forgotten sunglasses

You are more blind in the sun
than a snowman

I melt into wicked witch, at your feet
Reaching up to you
Stinging fingers full of kettle steam

Wishing I spoke coal
Or rock salt
Or silk hat
Or black Magic 8 Ball

Wishing I had a
candy heart
Wishing I was part
Blowtorch
Marshmallow
Or kerosene

Wanting to take you with me
Begging you to come along
and be a tsunami with me

Together we could have been
an ocean for so many, but

you prefer puddles

I will try again, tomorrow
when we become cloud,

again

Death of a Snowman
"What did the puddle say?" Lori McGinn

Puddle, what do you have to say
for the man who melted away?

What of his frozen heart
and the ice in his veins?
Did he have any last words,
or is this all that remains?

Did he beg for forgiveness?
Did he writhe in pain?
Did he confess all his sins
or mention my name?

Did he shed any tears?
Was he broken and shamed?
Was he left all alone
with no one to blame?

The one who vanished
in a duel with high noon
Whose shadow fell lifeless
under blazing doom

As the moon waxed on
he must have bled into the street
Was there anyone to comfort him?
Did anyone weep?

Did he look to the heavens?
Did he bargain for life?
Did he talk to his maker?
Did he finally see the light?

I pray he found peace
I hope he found grace
Tell me puddle that he left here
with a smile on his face

There Was No White

Not a frail dove wing
or a Velvet lily bloom

Nor sheet of snow
Or frigid breeze

No frozen apple cheeks
or icy-wet breath trapped in my lungs

No mercy of a womb

Only a Chrysalis,

Hope hangs
locked in a sealed tomb

No Deductions

The patch of mud
outside the door
didn't hold a single foot print
No men's tennis shoe-Size 11
None lead up to the porch, or away
No proof anyone had been there
The front door was shut
The closets were empty
Not even a forgotten white hankie lay flat
  on the back corner of the topmost shelf
Every cupboard is bare
Except for small mounds of sawdust,
Mostly the work of termites
No stray crumbs were being carried to an ant's hill
Not a single penny nail driven half into the stucco
  above an empty mantle
Not a stray eyelash on white tile
No soapy residue
No empty bottles covered in dust
No kite string caught in a tree
Or leather lace of a lost glove on the back porch
Not a single broken twig on the overgrown hedge
No sign of a struggle or hasty escape
No, none of those things...
I like to pretend
there was once a coffee table
growing dust around a family bible
Your cup at breakfast
Drinking black coffee
No one has yet to report any crimes, but

I can't stop investigating

Where did you go?

I cannot rest until I find some clues
into your disappearance
So I can do it, too

It Never Happened
and No One Can Prove It

We were free to be nobodies
There was nothing to see
Not the lack of a scarf
nor the absence of a haircut
Not a pair of blank pages
mirroring each other's nothing
We weren't the anonymous authors
of "untitled" titles
or the writers of wordless screenplays,
or poets un-reciting the un-repeatable
Songs weren't sung about unsung heroes
We didn't include pictures,
diagrams or dioramas
No film footage or DNA samples
No page numbers or punctuation was needed
No decimal points or average speeds were
calculated
There was nothing to document how non-existent
you felt
Or proof of you having had any effect on me
Or vice versa
It wasn't history
It couldn't be
Because no one even remembers
how it sadly never began
or how happily it never ended
No one knows what wasn't said while
No trees fell
No one saw or felt the kiss goodnight and

No one will ever relive the moment
Nothing was drunk or eaten
We didn't blink or think
Cough, sneeze, sniffle or take a breath
We were the essence of nothing
We weren't anywhere
and no one can disprove it.
Not even you.
You weren't there ...
Remember?

Good Cop/Bad Cop

I can't keep track of which side
of my brain is which
Because they are both so good at their job

One is a ruthless, lock jawed, drooling pit bull
licking my face
The other hugs with all the warm-fuzzy of a python
wrapped around my neck

You should see those two go at me
when they know I've been up to no good

I'm on their beat 24/7
They get paid triple time
even when I sleep

It's their job to lull me
into sense of decency
or trick me
into spilling my guts

I've been informed that all my words,
whether spoken or not,
can and will always will be
used against me
both in and outside a jury of my peers

Currently, I am cuffed to a warm coffee pot

With my only phone call, one of them suggested

a pizza and we couldn't agree on cheese
or pepperoni, or extra Pavulon

I will never leave this interrogation room

I'll be stuck behind this two-way mirror
for the rest of my life

Recovered Dental Records Will
Indicate Cause of Death:
Lack of a Heart

The full moon is still up this morning
scouring the city for a glimpse of you

My fingers are sore and my heart is full

Like Monet I painted haystack after haystack
because haystacks are like snowflakes
And you were a snowflake
I couldn't capture before melting away

I am a river, I never sleep

When I don't know what I think
I lose my softness
and become a brutal killer
who can handle a shovel

The last time I sat in this booth:
We were still friends
and I had an appetite

But Your loving detachment
felt too much like a tourniquet and a bread knife
You said, "I still love you" like a band-aid
And now you look like the victim
of a reckless weed whacker

I only wanted you to be—

drunk-in-love with me, again
If you were still here
I'd buy you a drink
or seven

Whiskey reminds me that you had a tongue
and I hate remembering that you had a tongue
And despite what the worldwide web says,
your elbows were totally lick-able

Last night, after you took your last breath
the frogs began to sing with voices so high
they pricked like pins

I stayed and watched the clouds, dumb as sheep,
clump together like cotton candy
hoping to recognize you among them
and imagined that being in the sky
must be like being in water

While walking on fossilized ferns and your DNA
another movie montage of us plays
on loop in my head

I liked it when we used to play kick ball
dodge ball, house or doctor
or some kind of game where we hit each other.

Now the labyrinth of roads we explored
slither around my ankles rubbing
and purring like a desperate lover—
begging me to return home
though our homes remain vacant

We were always somewhere in between
because you were not the same genre of
human as anyone else

You expected me to believe so many crazy
conspiracy stories:

Like aliens built the Capitol records building
You blamed the Challenger Explosion
on the freaks at NASA
for using Mc Nugget slime as adhesive

You were freaking crazy

My love,
you cannot be lost

I am blind

The moon is blind

Everyone is blind

Except the policeman at every intersection
plowing his brow into furrows
waiting for me
to give myself away

The Power of Then

the last time
I wanted to be me
I was with you

Dear, Lemon Drop

I sucked you down slowly
making you last
most of the morning

Melting you
into a smooth sliver
that glistened on the tip
of my tongue

I tried to savor
the last of your sweetness
and for that you cut my lower lip

But, that is not why I bit you

I bit you because
I always begin to miss you
long before you are gone

Where Are You Now?

The question is not rhetorical
Nor optional
Speak up
Draw a diagram
Break it down like I'm five
Ten times if you have to

Tell me exactly how you got there
What did you have you become to survive?

And, why?
Why did you have to go at all?

Tell me, again.
Only slower,
sweeter,
and sexier this time

Like you mean it

Look me in the eye
and beat me into dead horse
Drag me to a pool of the truth
Make sure I drown in it

Remember how rudder-less I am
Burn me to the hull

And Compass-less
Pray for quicksand between

the land mines
and know that I am down to a single beating wing
Bury the hollow bones alive if it survives

I'd spread it over the last of your

　listless..

　　and lifeless...

I would gladly fry
Just to shade you from the sun

I'd leap from the highest high
to get there

Give me a mark to aim for

You were once a lone snowflake

A lost hope,
like me

Mr. Blue

The breeze is so full of your exhale
I can catch it mid-air
when I let myself become still
long enough to feel

I can still hear your old fears
crow into my
Hummingbird ears
And I follow you deep
into every death defying leap

I pretend not to take
your mayday calls seriously
and say..."Don't look down...
we have nothing to lose
but our lives"

The whole truth is never
of interest to dare devils
like us

You said you were content
to be the anonymous wind,
So I dressed like a kite
to be held by you on a beautiful summer day

Prepared to dance and laugh and dance
And be twirled into a twisted tornado
of yellow jackets

But, now here I hang alone,
still and directionless as a dead leaf—
stuck up in a willow, weeping dirges
to the doldrums

I'd have become a nun,
full of black and white miracles
but you forsook God
and all your bad habits

Remember when I was the condor,
and you built a nest of
tumble weed, angel hair,
prayer and butterfly wing?

How could you rebuke a sky
so full of space?

Wasn't that all that ever you wanted?

I am still here
tangled up in my own tail
waiting on you to return
and give me
one more reason to fly

Wanted Dead

We'd bet that I would drown
in my glass half-full
before you could down
your nearly empty

We both refused to die thirsty

You like nothing better
than betting on losers
and lovers
who are willing to fall
for scotch on the rocks

The caliber that still believe in you
are all hollow point and sawed-off

Let's have another round of roulette
Russian rules, you demanded

Round and round I went
Where I stopped
You don't care
The now half-full chamber
No longer excites you

You only checked in
so you could check back out
Throw a few knives behind your back
while putting an apple
through the arrow in my mouth

I try to remind you
that you will lose me forever
One of these days I won't answer

You only smile
because you've never believed me

Despite what a great liar I am
nothing could be truer

Yes, I have cried wolf from the middle of a riptide
And screamed "Jaws!" in crowded theaters

I have waved a white flag
while running naked through a forest fire
of hunting seasons, just to tell you about it

I am not made of asbestos
and I am short a few life boats

When I look down
the tips of the icebergs
in my glass make me shiver

You tell me to dive in
as you prepare a toast
You brought butter and jelly
and a bottle of justice
to crack over my deepest bow-
then say you will wait for an autopsy
before you believe anything about me

Plotting Headstones

"Remember her
as the crazy one
who never gave up."

The one who stood
at the exit
to the cemetery
Waiting
in the pouring rain,
which came
and went
3 times an hour
but you
never did

I watched
And waited
Soaked and alone
through the night
In the dark
With nothing
but frozen ghosts
to console me

They called me crazy
and laughed
Just like you do, until
dawn when
a funeral party
crashed my

pity party

It all ended
hours ago

I am always
the first and the last
one mourning

It never feels
like a winning

From My Cell

Yes, the bloodstain on the carpet was my fault
I take full responsibility
I could have kept denying it, forever
But I can't live with my lies any longer
I cheated at everything, my whole life
Every board game, hand of poker,
  and crossword puzzle
I always finished the last of the milk
The coffee and the cereal
I lied to you at least once a day about something
Usually, nothing very important
I told people your deepest darkest secrets
And, I regret it in most cases
I am the one who ran over your dog
And, threw out your magazines
  after I spilled the last of the wine on them
It's my fault your credit is ruined and 24 Hour
Fitness will always be after you
I am the reason the floorboards bulge
I left the water on and the back door open
Sorry those guys got in and stole all your stuff
They were my friends and I told them not to
I am sorry for all of this and so much more
If it makes you feel any better—
I will likely face a firing squad at dawn
I'm going down for a crime
I'd never plan to commit

God Bless Us, Everyone

Bells of freedom ring
And wake me from my three worst nightmares

I am not chained to this bed

I throw back the curtains
and call down to
a boy in the street
to ask him what day it is

He proclaims
"it is the morning of
our saving grace's birth"

Which means:
I am not too late
YOU are not dead
and I need not be alone

Crippled and small
as you are...
I have let go of the coins clenched in my fists
just to hold up your head

As I dress for our cooked goose
I will sing from this windowsill
of my love for you
and this world

Though I want everyone to hear—

No one will care much

I owe the world a good laugh
after all that crying
and pitiful whining
and pining I've done

My song will always be sung
at the top of my lungs
out of key
on purpose
so you will recognize me

Gag Order

I choke on words
to keep them down
as they claw their way up to find you

They bring you no comfort

Though I want to wrap you in them,
like I used to

Coo you into morning, dove
Calm cool grey

I fear that my sack lunch notes
may never set well with you, again

My naptime whispers only
poke fun at your peace

Come bedtime, I still wish upon stars
to mesmerize you

To just once again Scheherazade
you with bedtime stories

My spinning mobile
lullaby, laser-light show has gone
from dim to dismal

I'd let you laze
between my sweet nothings—

for the rest of your life
if you only wanted to

I still whisper "I love you" across this great land

Let my words wander the whims
of ocean current and dessert dune

You used to listen for it
over the roar of stadiums

Now you'd cover your ears
and run screaming from the room,
if you only knew

I only want to kiss your dreams sweet
Say a prayer knelt at the foot of your bed
And lace milk and honey into your midnight

But that only makes you more prone to nightmares

My words are invisible elaborate silk
across the darkest doorways
Terror traps for the tired and hungry

All I can do for you
is to become one
with the silent night

The Waning Moon

Cannot speak
Cannot sleep
Cannot dream
Cannot wake
Cannot grow
Cannot fight
Cannot run
Cannot quit
Cannot cry
Cannot hide
Cannot die
Cannot love
Cannot forgive
Or remember to forget
I am no satellite
I can whisper
I only want to scream
I am a white lie
Caught in a black secret
Dying to give myself away

To the Un-forgiven

You prefer to sleep
on a bed of dry leaves
than ask for absolution

Shame is easier to maintain than love
Hiding feels safer than high ground

You only know how to take
the path you've always taken

The one that spirals
deeper and deeper
into the darkest places
of self loathing

I am learning to forgive the unforgivable in you

And the dirty, bearded tangle of me
begging to die on the cold street called you

Lessons In Gravity

You dropped an apple
on my head
If you had been a tree,
I would have understood

You dropped an apple
on my head
and called me names.
If you had been a howler monkey,
I would have understood

You dropped an apple
on my head,
called me names, and ran away
If you had been my enemy,
I would have understood

You dropped an apple
on my head,
called me names, ran away
and never came back

If you hadn't been my friend,
I would have understood

We Prefer Cold War

One day you will face me, again
with your fearful war paint on

You will not admit what a coward
you were and still are

I will go to my death
before I could ever confess
what a liar I have been

Yes, a traitor, friendly fire,
and the hand behind
the lobbed grenade

This time, my sweet time bomb
Not much will be said

I will not kiss you
hello or goodbye

I will not pick up a stone

But you will not kiss my cheek,
shake my hand,
or help me draft a treaty

You have convinced me that
truces are for quitters and losers

I dread this day more than you do

I wish you no shame or blame

It seems the best I can hope for
is that we both agree to disagree
for the rest of our lives

Promise to turn and walk away
without fully understanding
without completely forgetting
and without forgiving anything
just so the collateral damage
of our love can live on
to fight another day

Staying Cool

I take cold showers, every morning
and as often as needed
Then lie wet and naked on the linoleum tile
I run through sprinklers by day
and swim polar seas by night

On weekends I drive to the air-conditioned mall
Climate controlled library, chill in a matinee,
Or stay at home, turn out the lights and stand with
the freezer door open while sucking on ice

After the gym or a run, I bathe in a tub
of strawberry-banana smoothie
and watch snow on TV
All my meals are frozen confection, like
Choco Tacos, blizzards, and Baked Alaska

There are just too many
cool ways to stay cool
There just aren't enough
hot hours in the livelong day to do it all

I am so cool, the rest of the world feels
about a 451,000 degrees Fahrenheit
Like there are six suns on the horizon

But, I am a cucumber--
lying in the crisper drawer, half frozen
next to the iceberg lettuce
Waiting on a splash of cool and zesty

to become part of a healthy balanced brunch

My lips are always frosted— refreshing
as a cherry-cola Slurpee on a road trip
to the dark side of Mars

I wear all the hottest fashions
Made from the sheerest sheets of Popsicle
and chocolate pudding skin, fresh from the fridge
A sprig of mint is tucked behind each ear

These shoes have built in air conditioning
My feet are two bouquets of roses
Straight from the cooler at the floral shop
inside the grocery store

My head is a bottomless fuzzy brown coconut
filled with pure, white piña colada
under the shade of a colorful umbrella
31 flavors of fabulously frigid
with whipped cream, fresh snow
and a chilled silver spoon

But, the truth is I am even cooler than that
I am the new black, ice-ice baby
Blaring on the radio
Hydroplaning up the coast with the top down
Wearing your lost sunglasses
I am so cool
Don't come any closer
You will melt

Fashionably Late Regrets

You were obviously
a cool winter
While I am clearly
White-hot summer
You'd never suit my body type
They don't even make you in my size
You only made my ass
  look flatter and fatter at the same time
While causing chafing,
blisters, calluses, and excessive bleeding
Headaches, seizures, psychotic breaks, possible
death...Reckless leg syndrome,
Restless abandon, bad credit,
Anxiety, liver failure, and nuclear disaster
You would surely
Bind and buckle
Waffle and slip
Slide up before
tripping me over
knocking me down
and falling apart
and off.
Leaving me naked
on the street
in the worst part of town.
Another wardrobe malfunction waiting
to surrender and become
Unseemly red carpet litter
for the drama deprived

You would have been nothing
more than unsightly tan lines
accentuating my multiple muffin tops
and revealing every less than shapely shape

Sacrificing silhouette for kicks and spite

You mostly promised to bring sexy
back-fat, back

You would have forever cramped my style
So poorly designed and hastily constructed

Itchy

You'd have never survived my delicate-cycle

My only regret is not holding on to you
for the rest of my life

At the Station

I have been sitting
on this wooden bench
watching passengers
like you
come and go
for countless lifetimes
as if there
were endless tomorrows

I will spend this forever day
Like all the rest
Not wishing any of it away
Nor will I get the will
to move on,
carry on
Or, be on anything
Anywhere
Anytime
Ever,
again

From now on
I just "am"
all the time

I will watch you

You with your packed bags
You with your overstuffed—
everything

You and your stupid scarves
You and your handful of crumpled tickets
And loose change
Panicking your way through
a sea of mirror images of yourself
Determined
Lost and confused
Moving in every conceivable direction
and somehow all upstream
all at the same time

You may be hooked
But, you will get away
Just like you promised yourself
Just like everyone else
And then, I may never see you, again

If only I could convince you
to stop and stare
inside yourself
so you can see
that there is no place
more important
than being wherever
you are
right now

The Bridge I Rebuilt to You is Multiple Universes Wide

All of it is for you
Every rain forest creature
sea dweller and air breather
All the winged beasts and flying machines
The chocolate chip cookie
Beer
The ocean floor and shore
Plumeria blossoms,
sidewalks, ocean piers and park benches
Music
Poetry
The offbeat
Road trips. And road kill
Even The Police,
Extended dance mixes
Where babies come from,
And the concept of God
This has all been an elaborate scheme
to get you to fall in love with me again
Yes, I am responsible for the mid-east crisis
Disease, The Cure,
Global warming, tidal waves
And nuclear disasters
Every abuse of power
Every birth and death
since the beginning of time has
been a thread in a tangled web
woven to tickle your fears
and soothe you back into silk against my cheek

There would be no Jupiter without you
No golden, life-giving sun
I imagined it all
Just for you

Hoping these bodies
would bring you
close enough to touch

Where Has Our Love Been?

I loved you past the pain
Beyond the wet kisses
Along the well worn trail
And deep into the grizzly cave

I love you farther than the wolf howl
Taller, deeper, longer, wider and
with more wild-west lawless
than the middle of the Mohave
At midnight

I promise to love you beyond
the mysterious abandon
of Bermuda Triangle lost forever
after we are Ganges clean
Galapagos gifted
And Amazon twisted
From the depth
of Marianna's trenches
after a death defying
Himalayan climb

I will love you from
Mercury red
to Plutonian blue

Until there is only purple
And black hole true

The Evolution Of Harmony

You finally believe me
and I now understand you
till death do us part

We now feel each other's feelings
as if they were our own

We are in perfect agreement
about all that happened
and what has and hasn't been said

We know exactly who was at fault,
every time

With precise decision
we sorted out each detail
down to the infinitesimal
From the slightest impatient glance
and peppery tones
to the disregarded
damp sheets and salty pillowcases

It was split
smack dab down the middle,
exactly dead even
50/50
Every time
We weighed and measured,
added and divided
It came out exactly the same and

We are now certain,
even though we are both terrible at math,
we have nothing left to confess —

We are now as spring chicken
fresh plucked
juicy sweet delicious
as the day we first met

Your baritone has learned to dance
the Lambada and butterfly kisses
my soprano so sweetly

You are a Prince once again.
With all the shine of new car scent,
and concourse, muscle-car elegance

While I sparkle and shimmer
white as snow
under showroom light,
on black velvet smooth,
under polished glass night

A blue jay lands on my shoulder
You whistle and I hum

We have forgiven and forgotten
Our wishing well is still and deep

It only took us another lifetime
to return to this

The Weekend I Became a Yogi

I first learned to be as quiet and still
as an egg
hanging by the invisible
from the underside of a dark green leaf
Next, I learned to stretch
Slowly
To reach for the sun
And take deep breaths
Breath
After breath
And exhale after exhale
Soon only thanksgiving rose from my chest
I learned to push until the walls around me
crumbled
and fell and away
Only the roof gently cradled my delicate head
A wet fuzzy hatchling in me was born
a ball of newborn wiggle,
buzz and fuzz
I could feel the future of flight
filling within my hollow bones
I became 100 percent aware of being fully
articulated
I recall all 99 ungainly legs
with complete clarity
They possessed the strength of a thousand men
I travelled over endless hill and leaf
Living off the land
Devouring whatever nourishment the wild
provides becoming –

one with trees and earth
Almost touching the sky
Going blind
Getting fat on inner beauty and tranquillity
Next, I learned to fold all 99 arms in prayer at once
I was prepared for a great metamorphosis
Cocooning myself away
I grew wings
And God himself
Painted them the colour of me
I learned to let go of the branches
I have learned to flutter and fly
I have no fear of falling
Or being eaten alive

Our Love Will Forever Be Home to Someone

Our smoke ring secrets escaped
Pandora's burning box
and survived long enough
to send a message to the rain clouds
who whispered all of our mysteries to the seeds
who become so fat on our story
they burst into a forest of gnarled branches,
laden with nests of chirping baby birds—
a haven to honeybee and squirrel
painted ladies and the generations of monarchs
who will flit around the fruit of our lost love
and spread it to the rest of creation

The End

❄

About the Author...

Raundi Kai Moore-Kondo grew up in sunny Southern California praying for white Christmases and daydreaming about making the perfect snowman. Her loving parents wisely forbade her from leaving the front yard and chasing after the first snow flurry that fell from the sky. Eventually, she hit the road, met her fair share of snowmen, became a poet, and this is the book she built.

Raundi became many things she once only dreamed of being: Including a wife, mother, teacher, rock star, fiction writer, publisher, singer/songwriter, author of <u>Let The Ends Spill Over Your Lips</u>, and The Founder of *For the Love of Words Creative Writing Workshops & Small Press*

When she isn't pushing poetry on people Raundi is bassist and singer for the bands Hurt & the Heartbeat and Daisy Unchained.

www.TheLoveOfWords.com

Acknowledgements:

Thank you, to the greatest loves of my life
Michael, Savanah and Harrison
This book and too many other things would not exist
without you.

And to my dear friend the poet, Lori McGinn,
who asked...

"What did the puddle say?"

❄

www.ingramcontent.com/pod-product-compliance
Lightning Source LLC
Chambersburg PA
CBHW071239090426
42736CB00014B/3145